Finding a Job in Tough Times

by
Dr. Tim Johnson, DPS, PE
Captains Engineering Services
400 2nd Avenue
NY, NY 10010

Printed in the United States, by Lightning Source, Inc.
1st Edition, June 2002
2nd Edition, May 2006
3rd Edition, December 2018
4th Edition, April 2019
5th Edition, September 2019
6th Edition, December 2019
7th Edition, February 2020

Other Books by the Author
    History of Open-Water Marathon Swimming, 2005
    Introductory Digital Logic Labs, 2007
    Performance Sailing on a J29, 2007

Plays Written by the Author
    Stud of the Hudson—A Swim in Twenty Stages, 2006

Editor: Robert Young, PhD

Cover design: "Seashore", a watercolor by Avery Johnson, age nine.

Publisher:
Captains Engineering Services
400 2nd Avenue, 23B
New York, NY 10010

COPYRIGHT © 2002 Captains Engineering Services
All rights reserved. No part of this book may be reproduced, in any form or by any means, without the permission in writing from the publisher.

ISBN 0-9721726-0-2

Dedication

This book is dedicated to the many individuals who will pick this book up and make the effort to complete the exercises in the belief that the principles outlined herein are worthy of adopting in their own lives and will make a difference in their job search outcomes. While the specific times they begin this reading and study might be low points in their life, it is with the hope that the changes the principles are focused upon will happen because they are universal and beneficial to the nature of mankind. Who among us when asked for help would not see what they could do? To be asked is a great honor that inspires us to become a better person, one who strives to be the best possibly person that is within us to become.

Contents

INTRODUCTION 3
- WHO ARE YOU? 5
- WHAT HAVE YOU BEEN THROUGH? 9
- WHAT DOES THE FUTURE LOOK LIKE? 13
- WHAT HAPPENED? 15
- WHY ME? 19
- NEGATIVES 21

SIX STEPS TO A PAYCHECK 23

REDEFINE YOURSELF 25
- INVENTORY TIME 27
- SELF-KNOWLEDGE 29
- WHO ARE YOU? PART 2 33
- REDEFINE YOUR GOALS 37
- THE NEXT GOAL 41
- THE DIFFERENCES BETWEEN A WISH AND A GOAL ARE PLANS 45

REEXAMINE LIMITATIONS 49
- NO-LIMITS LIVING 51
- AND THE BIBLE SAYS… 53

CREATE OPPORTUNITIES 55
- A SHORT STORY ABOUT KEEPING FRIENDS 57
- A LONGER STORY ABOUT MAKING NEW FRIENDS ... 59
- WHERE ARE THE JOBS? 61
- WHERE DID THE JOBS GO? 63
- WHAT'S THIS ABOUT GOING WITH THE FLOW? 65
- IF THE PART IS BROKEN, THERE ARE CHOICES… 67

NEVER SAY NO 69
- LIFE ISN'T PLANNED 71
- ENJOY 73

FOCUS 75
- DETAILS—RESUME 77
- DETAILS—INTERVIEWS 81
- STAY FOCUSED 83
- CHANGES 85
- A SYSTEM SOLUTION 87

SUMMARY: SIX STEPS TO A PAYCHECK 91
- LIST OF EXERCISES 93
- ABOUT THE AUTHOR 95

Introduction

This book is not a novel. There are no characters to meet but yourself. There are principles that I will be communicating to you in the form of a plan that you can implement in a step-by-step fashion. We'll be doing exercises and working on ideas, so think of this more as a workbook.

For the reading of this book to be successful, you'll have to do a little work. You're going to be taking a class; I'll be instructing you. You won't hear my voice speaking to you. You'll hear your voice reading my words. My lectures consist of ideas to help you find a job. Since I normally teach electronics to young adult males, I address this topic from that perspective. The principles and ideas I present apply equally well to everyone. I'll be asking you questions and testing you by assigning you exercises as if you were in school. You can use the space I've provided for you or use your own notebook to write your answers.

To get the most out of the lessons, do the exercises. I suggest that you purchase a stenographer's notebook, the pages of which flip over the top. Label the start of a new exercise with its name and the date you began. The notebook can become a journal where you include what else is going on in your life, accomplishments, and other ideas that might flash through your mind as you work on the exercises. The information derived early on is used in later exercises, so don't skip anything. Answers you provide may be quite useful when you prepare your resume. You may take a while to complete this book. When you do, you'll be well on your way, secure in a career path that will make you a happy and successful person.

Reading this book and completing the exercises is like taking a special class because you are my only student. And you have the luxury of going over every word carefully to extract every bit of meaning out of what I'm saying to you. My chapters are not long because I am not going to talk you into a job; once I think the point is made, questions are provided for your input. If you consider the exercises as a workout, you are getting in shape for your job. For this book to have the maximum effect, you *must* write down your answers to the exercises. If you are haphazard or vague, the technique of self-direction will not work as well as is possible. The plan presented in this book will assist you in your job search, because you are going to personalize it.

Perhaps you are interested in a promotion. There are different types of job changes: lateral moves, territorial transfers, and promotions. The preparation after you decide to put your name forward is much like applying for the same job from outside the organization. All the principles covered for finding a job apply toward getting a promotion. The key for a promotion is to stand head and shoulders over your coworkers, but for a smooth transition, the support of your coworkers is essential.

This book is my effort to assist those that want or need a little more help in their job search. Not everyone can process the information at the same rate, but everyone can reach a level of understanding that will put their world in better perspective.

On the website www.findingajob.net is a blog that allows the author to address current issues in employment, a free PowerPoint covering *Six Steps to a Paycheck*, a calendar, and a point of contact for your questions.

Who Are You?

A recent college graduate. A member of a minority group. A laid-off technology worker. Regardless, you're looking for a job—a good job. One where you can show off your talents and bring home a little bacon.

To get a job, you must know who you are. That might sound insane—of course, you know who you are. But could you describe yourself?

This is a crucial aspect of job hunting that will take some thought. Not everyone can step back to look at themselves without prejudice. To help you, I'm going to ask you to describe someone else. If you were asked to describe a favorite teacher, you might start with their name; then you'd describe characteristics about them that are easily observable. If you'd like more room than is available in this book, utilize a notebook. Complete the following exercise by writing down the exercise number, date, and the title.

Exercise 1: Describe Your Favorite Person

1. Time to break out the notebook. While you are doing that, think about who you would write about and what you would say.
2. You are not limited to one person.
3. Please complete this exercise before going on.

Did you describe your teacher physically? Did you describe other types of characteristics? Did you mention anything special about them? Who *you* are can be described by these same clearly defined categories. You're a man, a woman, a teenager, or a senior. You would be tall, short, overweight, or thin. While these are physical characteristics, they help in describing who you are. Personality is the next easiest. *Funny*, *stern*, *intelligent*, *caring*, and *understanding* would be some descriptive words that characterize a person you admire.

How would you describe yourself? Complete the following exercise by making two columns, one for your physical appearance and another for your personality:

Exercise 2: **Self-Description**
1. Physical description
2. Personality

How did you do with this exercise? Which was easier to complete: the physical side compared to the personality side? Was one list longer than the other? Do you have more than three for each? If you don't have at least five for each, try going back later after more thought. Was it easier to write about someone else, as in Exercise 1?

The reason for this exercise is simple: you need to be able to look at yourself from the perspective of the employer. *If you were sitting across the table from yourself, what would you see*? One of the important tools in the hiring process is the personal interview. Here you sit down with an employer and talk about their position, and your qualifications, and you get a chance to learn about their company. During an interview, physical descriptions are quickly determined in the first thirty seconds. Evaluating how your personality would fit in their company will take a little longer. Suppose you were to interview yourself. Could you, from a five-minute conversation (with yourself) determine the personality traits that you have written down in the exercise? Do your answers for Exercise 2 reflect what this paragraph suggests? If not, go back and include them in the list.

Another way to check what you have written is to ask someone you know (a friend) to write a description of you. Their description might help you to see yourself in a different way and uncover words you see as unimportant or bragging. Remember, nothing you've written is final; change is always possible.

Physical and personality traits are simply ways of categorizing you. Who is doing the categorizing? The employer! The employers list their expectations in job descriptions. During the interview, employers make one crucial decision: to hire you or not. You need to get a sense of who they are seeing when you apply for a job. If you can meet their expectations, they will hire you. If you can get them to consider you for the position, they might hire you. The interview is your opportunity to show them that even though you might be different from their expectations, you can do the work required for the position.

All an employer knows about you at the start of the interview comes from a piece of paper with your name, a history of your education, and your work experience. They don't know who you are, but they do know what you've done. The interview is their opportunity to get to know you. They'll ask you questions about what you've done and why you left a past employer. These are hard questions to answer, but employers are interested in how you react to situations when you are under pressure. They are just getting a feel for how you are to work with. During this interview process of questions and answers, they get an insight into you, the person. Hopefully, at the end of the interview, their description of you will match yours.

What Have You Been Through?
A seemingly endless round of interviews. A diminishing list of possibilities. While your background isn't outstanding, neither is it without merit. You're proud of where you've been and hopeful for the future.

As a young man, I was also unemployed and searching for work. This wasn't a pleasant experience. I swore everyone on the subway train knew I was unemployed. I could spot another unemployed person at a glance. Their newspaper was open to the want ads (well before Monster and other online job search apps). I imagined a giant neon sign was floating over my head reading, UNEMPLOYED. Since I was the head of a small new family, I especially felt like a failure.

There are two reasons I share these feelings with you. One is because nearly everyone now working has been in the same position. This is the reason people hang onto a lousy job with an awful boss. They never want to feel that way again. They would do anything to avoid those awful feelings, but life happens.

The second reason is to let you know there is a difference between feelings and actions. Your actions will get you a job. On the positive side, let's say you go to an interview. You fill out another application. You take a test. You wait around. Someone talks to you, and then you wait to hear. No one can see your feelings. They are that little something extra that lets you know you're alive. Being alive is that wonderful moment when you realize how important you are. This can happen when you share your life with someone else who loves you, or when you watch a sunrise. It's a wonderful, joyous feeling that is indescribable and fills your being with happiness.

When you are feeling rejected, blue, or alone, can be just as overwhelming as the happiness. The feeling of rejection comes with a judgment, a self-assessment of an outcome when compared to an ideal or expected outcome. Both feelings come with messages: one is encouragement and self-congratulation, and the other is discouraging and critical. Both messages could be wrong or not capturing the whole truth. In a simplistic manner of reasoning, a wonderful view from a mountaintop is surrounded by valleys.

You also must be fully human to appreciate these feelings. I wouldn't want to miss a feeling, because they are what make me unique. I appreciate myself in an authentic way. An authentic person doesn't need drugs to handle daily life. You don't need a drink or cannabis to feel better or be happy. If you do, you may need to resolve some issues beyond just finding a job.

I can remember as a young man setting my sights on going to Annapolis. When I heard the news that I wasn't selected, I was devastated. I went to the pool to go swimming, and a friend asked me if I had heard anything. I felt angry, so I yelled at him. I dove in as if the surface of the water was covered with burning oil, and I had to get under the water quickly. Even the water annoyed me. I threw my strokes like I was punching the water. Guys will do anything to avoid crying. I was fine the next day—a little lost but okay. A few years later, I realized I needed to let go of those feelings.

This is a rather long sermon on feelings, so let's get to the exercise. This is a hard one. I want you to write down how you feel when you are rejected. Try to remember a situation when you felt rejected or unwanted.

In Exercise 3, write down enough about a situation when you were rejected to recall the feelings. The idea here is to recall the feelings, not the blame or opinions about other people involved, just *how you felt* at the time. When you are completing the exercise, you may have to be a little detached and analytical. Pick something that happened in the past that might have a bearing on your career choices.

Exercise 3: Talking about Feelings
1. I felt rejected when…
2. This is how I felt then…
3. This is how I reacted…
4. This is how I feel today…
5. What would I do differently?

What Does the Future Look Like?

In a word: Bleak.

The future is only bleak if you let it be that way. It doesn't have to be. You might be letting your feelings get in the way of your life. Ever watch those movies where they talk about a parallel dimension? Well, every moment of every day is an instant where we can split off into these parallel dimensions (think science fiction and Hollywood). I'll choose the dimension with the swimming pool and Mercedes and so on. My past doesn't lock me in to my future. I am constantly choosing my life's direction. My circumstances have put me in a specific world. I can't change the past (my circumstances), but I can set about changing what's coming up next. If you think about life as a TV channel, you don't have to watch only one channel; you can change the channel. You hold the remote control for your life in your hands, and I am about to tell you how it operates.

Now for the two-question exercise. In the first part, think of a situation in your life that you'd like to do over. Briefly describe the situation and the outcome. For the second part, the more important part of this exercise, describe how you'd handle the same situation today.

In this exercise we learn that we are not trapped by our past and with a little understanding we can make better choices. The understanding is coming.

Exercise 4: Talking about the Past
1. What happened?
2. How would you change the outcome?

What Happened?
For the recent college graduate: Coming out of an academic situation into the business world requires you to adjust. Problems can't be solved within an hour. Your first "real job" is to nail down that first job.

College doesn't really prepare you for a career. There are no lessons that any teacher can prepare that could possibly encompass everything that you need to know to get through life. Schools give you some tools, the most important being the ability to think and reason so that when life presents you with a problem, you'll have the skill and ability to address the issue with confidence. Schools try to measure your skills and abilities in courses and thus give you a grade. This is a limited assessment and has no more finality or authority than the diploma given to the scarecrow character in *The Wizard of Oz*. Your diploma is what you make of it. You can take the diploma to your first job, rest on your laurels—and you know what? You'll never really get anywhere. You'd be better prepared for your first job if you pretended you didn't have a diploma and you had to earn your job by proving your ability and skills are worthwhile to your future company. This is a job strategy.

The exercise for this chapter is for you to list your abilities and skills. Let's define again what we mean by abilities and skills. If you can write a computer program in C++, that is *ability*. The *skill* is how well you perform the task. Introductory courses at college introduce you to some abilities that become skills when you take advanced courses. Being proficient at math, such as calculus, is an ability, but being able to apply that knowledge in a practical problem is a skill. I spent a career in the phone company and never once had to solve one problem using calculus. But math courses such as statistics, algebra, and graphing gave me some very common abilities that improved my skills to solve problems, and I called upon them all the time. Taking English classes gave me writing and communication abilities. Studying literature gave me the skill to write well. Taking history gave me the skill to reason, public speaking the skill to debate and make a point. Playing sports gave me the ability to work together on a team. I learned firsthand about teamwork. The ability to work on a team is very important on a job, and my skill level improved with every different sport I went out for. Studying navigation and seamanship taught me how to plot a position and maintain a vessel in shipshape condition. Skills developed by these courses are leadership, personal responsibility, and management.

In Exercise 5, make four columns. In the first row, label the columns as follows: course, what was taught, what you learned, and skill level attained. In the first column, write down the name of the courses that will highlight your abilities and skills. Senior projects (capstones) are a demonstration of your abilities and skills, so look closely at what you did and learned in that course. You might need a second page for this exercise, but some employers may be quite interested in your project.

I've provided a separate exercise in the next chapter that will suit older and more experienced employees better than this exercise, which is more suited for the recent graduate without job experience. The comparisons are laid out in column format so that you can identify which course was the source of your ability and skill. You can lay your transcript down and ask yourself: What did I learn in this course? Having this written down will help you fill the dead air in an interview. Start the conversation with, "My favorite course in college that helped me look into this career was…"

Pick some courses you liked and have been helpful to you. When you review what you've written, your favorite subjects should be obvious. You could have more than one; check back later to see if anything is missing from your list.

Exercise 5: Abilities and Skills (For the Graduate)
1. List the course, what was taught, the abilities you learned, and the skill level you achieved.

Now for the important question and the reason for this exercise: **Does your resume list these abilities and skills?** These are what should be apparent to the employer when they read your resume. These abilities and skills are what could make you a valuable employee to this company. Should you have no job experience, your abilities and skills are what are going to make you distinct from anyone else. You knew why you went to school, and you had a focus. Don't forget that mentioning your attendance can be helpful. If you never missed a class, say so. Even if you didn't finish college, you've had the experience, so you might want to discuss some aspects of one or two of your courses.

Why Me?

For the minority or the technology worker: it's not your fault. Economic conditions force managers to make decisions. They'd rather keep everyone and be thinking about hiring more personnel. They spent time and money training you, an investment that you now get to spend somewhere else.

This chapter is very similar to the previous chapter, except that for the individual with work experience, the exercise is slightly different. Here's the difference: you spent time learning skills, except you didn't always have a classroom instructor, and you were expected to learn a lot on your own. In your mind, go over in your mind what you learned and write that down. If you worked on a project, you were part of a team. Teamwork requires communication skills. The portion of the project you were responsible for is an indication of your abilities. The skill is how well you could accomplish that task. When you first started out on your job, you weren't as skilled or as knowledgeable as you are now. These skills that you practiced are what I want you to capture for this exercise and eventually put on your resume. Make four columns.

Exercise 6: Abilities and Skills (For the Worker)

1. Write who your employer was, the job function, the abilities you learned, and the skill level (competence) you achieved.

Negatives

While we've looked at what you learned on your jobs and what you have to offer, there may be some drawbacks. What are the reasons for your current job search? If you were laid off, was the reason because you were the least productive individual, or was the entire department terminated? This topic is not what you put on your resume; rather, expect this information to be solicited during the interview. Be prepared to address this issue.

You should be aware that when a company does a reference check, they will make inquiries of your previous employers to learn the cause of the dismissal. Should this be the case, if, during your unemployment period you dealt with and resolved the cause, then expect that this will become a nonissue.

This is to help you handle possible issues that may have occurred during your employment. Remember that a negative for one employer may not be a negative for another. For instance: If your family needs require you to be home every night, this is a red flag for a job with a 10 percent travel requirement.

Exercise 7: Negatives
1. What concerns would an employer have about your work history?
2. Have these issues been resolved if they should arise again?

Now that we've thoroughly discussed what you have to offer an employer, we're going to look at a plan that will put you where you want to be.

Six Steps to a Paycheck

- *Redefine Yourself*
- *Redefine Your Goals*
- *Reexamine Limitations*
- *Create Opportunities*
- *Never Say No*
- *Focus*

These six steps are a plan that allows you to look at yourself, your goals, your limitations, your opportunities, your motivation, and finally, your determination. We'll go over each one of these steps in subsequent chapters. This plan is not something that you can complete in one day, a week, or even within a month. This might take years due to interruptions. The exercises that help you develop the plan can be completed and refined over time. The plan is to make you the best person you can possibly be. This will not happen overnight.

Redefine Yourself

Getting into college was a big deal, but the day you walked off the campus with a college diploma was a triumph. You persevered over many obstacles. Let's look at that person.

What makes you employable? To assess this, we will take an inventory. You should know yourself so well that you could become the national spokesperson for yourself. You'll recognize priorities in your life and how you reached this point. You'll recognize patterns in your life that you can point to with pride. You'll be able to identify strong points that are characteristic of you because of your past history.

This is a critical look at your past. You have had a successful past that you can point to with pride, but you need to define your history in terms that makes sense to a prospective new employer. Let's look at some words that could define you: dependable, take-charge, team player, idea man or woman, consistent, achiever, go-to guy or gal, detail oriented, meticulous. Consider the way you have worked with other employees or customers and what you contributed to the effort.

The exercise for this chapter consists of three parts: what you were doing, what you contributed, and a trait. While this exercise is like Exercises 5 and 6, to identify your abilities and skills, don't limit yourself to just your college or job experience. Consider any church, community, team, or athletic participation. Maybe you were a Little League coach, or maybe you organized a social outing for coworkers. Activities such as these identify traits that go beyond abilities and skills.

Exercise 8: Identifying Traits (Three columns)
  1. What you did / What you contributed / Trait
  2. List examples.

A trait is a characteristic or quality about you that this activity exemplifies. These traits become the *key words* that will help define *you* on your resume.

Inventory Time

What have you been doing since school? What have you learned that is new? What learning have you applied? Have you been working out at the gym? How have you been pushing yourself?

Resting on your laurels with too much free time to fill? If you're not working for someone else, you could show that you are working on yourself. Basically, the exercise for this chapter is to answer the five questions above. Imagine you were so famous that you had a national spokesperson who would explain your every action. Your spokesperson will want to know the answer to these questions because these are some of the topics that he'll be talking about. Your spokesperson might ask you if you have a list of books you've read. If you don't know what book to read, stop by any bookstore and pick up any history book or biography (not about Hollywood or people who are famous just for being famous). Read real stories about real people.

A person who maintains a personal schedule keeping busy and involved is just the kind of person employers are looking for. The employer needs to know they can count on you to show up, contribute, and work as a team member. They may want to know if you have a health problem and how that is working out. Join a gym and start doing some workouts. An alternative solution that is probably cheaper is to use those running shoes and start walking or training for a local five-mile run. You'll meet people who are training regularly, have specific goals in mind, and have a healthy outlook on life. People looking for a job have a lean look about them. They are ready to tear into their first assignment. Speaking of assignments, break out your pencils.

Exercise 9: What's New

1. Since my last job, I've been busy…
2. New knowledge (something I didn't know before)
3. What have I done with this learning?

There's more to you than what we've covered so far. You are a physical being, and as the owner of this fine biomechanical structure you have been entrusted with, what have you been doing to maintain the equipment in good working order?

Exercise 10: What's New, Continued

1. My workouts consist of…
2. I've also been doing the following…
3. Have you set any goals? Please list them here.

Self-Knowledge

In an interview, the employer is first concerned you can do the job (or can learn the job). Your degree and your experience answer that question.

Next, the employer wants to know about you. Only you can tell him about yourself. To do that, you must know yourself.

At this point, you can compare the traits you identified in Exercise 8 with the personality you filled out in the self-description in Exercise 2. Are they different? They should be. You've done more work at this point, and the information you revealed in the first exercise probably wasn't as well thought out. You might have been in a bit of a hurry to get into the meat of the material. The traits are based on a close look at what you've been doing. Here's how you're going to pull everything together.

You are…

- What you've done (your work history)
- Your abilities and skills
- What you are doing now
- Identifiable traits

Polish up your information from your previous exercises and put them into order in the following exercises.

Exercise 11: What's Your Experience?

1. Dates
2. Employers
3. Job functions you've handled

Repeat through to your last job.

Exercise 12: Your Abilities and Skills
1. What you've learned.
2. What you can do.

Exercise 13: What Are You Doing Now?
1. List current activities.

At this point, if you have trouble completing an exercise, you could go back and review your answers to previous exercises.

Exercise 11 is your work history. If you do not have work experience, this exercise will be empty. You can compensate with a list of abilities, skills, and extracurricular or volunteer activities.

In Exercise 12, you'll want around five items for the abilities and skills that are related to your work experience and more to branch out into other areas. Remember abilities are what you've learned, and skills are how well you can apply your learning.

Complete Exercise 13, "What Are You Doing Now?" from what you filled out in Exercises 9 and 10, "What's New?" Instead of giving the details as in those exercises, generalize the information. You are not "training for a five-mile run," you are "staying in shape" or "jogging."

The identifiable traits you'll list below in Exercise 14 are very important. They are the impressions you want to leave the interviewer to consider. You can't have too many, because a long list could be confusing to an interviewer, so go with your strongest traits. Be prepared to talk about them.

Exercise 14: Identifiable Traits

1. List five traits for yourself.

Who Are You? Part 2
What are your values? How many times have you been to the movies? How many times have you been to church? If you are living at home, are you helping out? What books have you read? You know yourself better than anybody.

These are good questions that are looking for balance in your life. Who you are to an employer is not isolated from who you are as a person, a family member, and a citizen. These broader aspects of you are considered in this chapter. In the following four exercises, I'd like you to look at the role you fill within a very familiar scene: your home. To help you with these exercises, I've written leading questions to help you focus.

Describe what you would do on a typical day at home:

> What time do you normally get up? Go to bed?
> Are you getting enough sleep?
> Do you have any chores?
> Do you have a list of items to accomplish?
> How much television do you watch?
> What has changed with being unemployed?
> Can you recall any accomplishments?
> What new skills have you learned?

Exercise 15: Life Assessments, Part 1
1. Describe your typical day at home from waking up to going to bed.
2. When is crunch time?
3. How do you help those who live with you?

Describe your roles at church/volunteer events:

>Do you attend church or do volunteer work?
>Do you help with activities?
>Have you made friends at these activities?
>Do you stay for the coffee hour and socialize?
>How could you better contribute to these activities?

Exercise 16: Life Assessments, Part 2
1. Describe your spiritual/community self.

What do you do to relax or enjoy yourself?

>List your favorite sports you participate in?
>How often do you do this?
>What is your view of exercise?
>What kinds of games do you like to play?

Exercise 17: Life Assessments, Part 3
1. Describe how you relax and enjoy your time.
2. Have you been injured in sports?
3. Are you overweight?

How do you make your role as a citizen real?

> Have you registered and voted?
> Have you signed a petition?
> Have you helped in a community project?
> Have you donated time to a service group?
> Have you attended hearings about an issue?
> Would your neighbors want you as a neighbor?

Exercise 18: Life Assessments, Part 4
1. How have you been as a citizen?

Each of these exercise questions is designed to help you look at who you are. They allow you to get a fuller picture of your life and the roles you played so far. You might discover that there are some vacant spots, roles you haven't explored. You might discover some areas where you could grow. For our purposes, we are looking for those traits to give an employer an idea of who you are and a reason to hire you.

Review your answers to the questions in the last few exercises and see if you could describe yourself and your activity using a single-word description. Would the word *involved* apply? Committed, casual, serious, caring, dedicated, friendly, and neighborly are other words that might come to mind in describing who you are to an employer. Some employers have no interest in your outside activities, but community-minded employers will. Some companies realize their employees aren't just employees from 9:00 a.m. to 5:00 p.m. but that they will be representing their company to people in the community twenty-four hours a day. This is a vital source of goodwill for their company. Incorporate any traits you discover about yourself in the last few exercises with your list from

Exercise 14. In the following exercise, reorder these revised traits in order of importance that you value the most.

Exercise 19: Revised Traits

1. List your traits.

Redefine Your Goals
What are your goals, now? Getting into college was the first goal. Graduating from college was the second. What's next? Have you set a new goal yet? Start dreaming. Real goals start out as wishes.

Some people only wish they had a job. They are not too particular. This book isn't for them. The job is only a means to an end. The end is for you to achieve your goals in life. This takes work, dedication, and insight to persevere through many setbacks. Everybody has setbacks. The important thing is to have a goal that you are focused on. In the PowerPoint presentation found on the book's website, I suggest what could be two goals that you might have had: 1) getting into a college, and 2) graduating from college. You might have reached these goals, but neither of these goals are a job. They were your job at the time. You went to school so you could learn enough to pass the tests to get into college. Then, in college, you had to take various courses to accumulate enough credits to graduate. Maybe you didn't finish. But at this point, you need a job, and having the job will make achieving your goals possible.

You need to know what you would like to be or do. You need to decide which way you are going to direct your life. You're not a kid anymore. This is a real-world wish, because once you decide, there's every probability that you will achieve this goal. The exercise for this chapter is going to take a little bit longer because you'll need to really think about what you want to become. Not everyone formulates the answer immediately. You need to put your ideas for yourself into your thinking cap and see what comes out.

As a young man, I remember sitting on a stack of lumber on a dock in California making just such a decision. I had been training to become a merchant marine officer, and after about eight months of my sea year, I had learned enough about the industry to decide if this career was what I wanted to do with my life. It wasn't. I didn't have a clear plan of what to do next, but I knew what I wasn't going to do. I decided in the negative, but that worked just as well. Knowing what I didn't want to do moved me along and helped define what I did want to do. Everything will become much simpler and clearer after you make the decision about what you want to do in your life.

What do you base the decision on? The answer varies, depending on your background and whom you know. If you had an uncle or family friend whom you admired, who was a firefighter, police officer, or a soldier, then you can't go wrong emulating their choice for a career. In looking over my family history, I had several relatives who became doctors, nurses, or served in the military. I didn't follow any of their careers. I went where my talents and interests were best served. The process did take me some time to find them. If you can figure out what you do best and then identify an industry that utilizes these talents, you'll be way ahead of me.

So, look at the traits you've used to describe what you do and use them as your guide. Hobbies and interests are good indicators of your talents. There may be an allied industry which could use the skills you have developed to help you make a living. I've done that more than once in my life.

I became intrigued by radio as a child, making a crystal radio with my dad. I later became a Federal Communications Commission licensed radio technician for the phone company, setting up microwave links and repairing and testing microwave equipment. I learned to sail at the US Merchant Marine Academy and sailed boats for my enjoyment as I grew older. After retiring at age forty-six from the phone company, I became a US Coast Guard licensed captain and worked regularly during the summer teaching people to sail and how to navigate. Both positions were dream jobs.

In the exercise for this chapter, I'd like you to consider what would be your ideal, dream job.

Exercise 20: Make a Wish
1. I want to be a...
2. Because...

What you write here may not be your next job. You may not be able to start this desirable position for some time. You might have to gain some experience in preparation. You might have to do some studying. But unless you know where you are going and have some direction, you may not recognize when an opportunity happens.

Have a goal in mind. This Wish Exercise is where you write down your goal. Then you read what you have written to see if it makes sense. A test of time can be employed by sleeping on your choice. This is where you began to formulate plans for your future. I've done this more than once in my life and achieved every one of them. My congratulations on your first step in becoming what you want to be.

The Next Goal
Athletes: When they achieve a goal they've worked for all their lives; they often don't know what to do next in their lives. They are unprepared; they are in a letdown. They haven't started training for their next goal. You have this unique opportunity to decide what your next move will be. You think life just happens…

This is a great opportunity for you. You're unemployed and you have the freedom to change your life. You get to pick what you'll be doing next—not your boss! This is an important decision, and I'd like you to be properly prepared to make this decision. You can start by going to the local library or go online to begin researching careers. There are all kinds of literature about different careers at the library, and they go begging for readers most of the time. This is your job: find out as much as possible about the career you are thinking about or one you have already decided upon.

Ask yourself questions. What do you need to know to become a CPA? What do you need to learn to go into the medical industry? Can anyone be a chef just because they worked at a fast-food place? What would the advantage be for getting specialized training for a career? Who gives this training? How could you cover the cost for the training? There is a world of information waiting for you to. Many states maintain websites for the unemployed. These sites list training and workshops for specialized help, so check them out. You may find out you qualify for benefits and free training.

In the last chapter, I asked you to make a wish. In this chapter, you are doing the hard work of finding out what you must do to make your future come true. Your assignment is to research *careers* (with the emphasis on the plural). In the beginning, you need to consider diverse goals. This can help you distinguish what it is that is attractive to you about a particular career and assist in the decision process. Pick three careers.

Exercise 21: Career Comparison

For each career, in each column, answer the following questions:

1. Name of the career
2. Education required
3. Experience required
4. Training required
5. Special knowledge/skills required
6. Any age requirements

This is the best part: try and decide which one you are best suited for. The research can also turn up more ideas. *Never pick a goal that is too easy.* You may notice one career looks challenging, but It could take some time to achieve. You'll want something to occupy you for the rest of your life. This something is going to challenge your best efforts in a career you can be proud of achieving.

Now the next part of this assignment is a little tougher. Get out the newspapers (or go online) and look up jobs in these careers. Here are the real-world criteria that you don't find in books. You'll get an idea what starting pay is, what the chance for advancement is, and whether there are any job openings at all in the industry. Some of this can be intimidating, much like learning to swim when you're peering into the deep end. You are not going there yet. You need an entry level position.

For the next exercise, select a starting job for each career for comparison purposes. One smart choice would be to pick a position in an allied industry. Here's what I mean by allied: people who trained as pharmacists as their career choice often wind up in the pharmaceutical industry as drug representatives. Both industries require similar training and basic knowledge, such as remembering and pronouncing the name of drugs/pills correctly as well as their intended usage. Just in case you need a backup career, you are prepared and will understand what the transition will require.

Exercise 22: Job Comparison

For each career, from Exercise 21 answer the following items:

1. Name of career
2. Position selected
3. Starting pay
4. Location
5. Requirements
6. Advancement
7. Advantages

The third part of the assignment is tougher still. You need to meet someone working in the industry and discuss *what it is like to work there*. If you don't know anyone in the industry, then you will want to visit a job fair where this industry is represented. You'll meet the human resources people who work for the industry. They are not quite the same as a worker, but they have some knowledge and can give you some good advice. You'll basically be interviewing the person you meet about their job or the industry. The way to conduct an interview is to ask interesting questions the person to whom you are talking would like to answer. In Exercise 23 are some questions which will help you gather information you'd probably want to know.

Exercise 23: Personal Interview

1. Whom did you meet? What is their position in that industry?
2. When and how did they get started?
3. What do they like about their job? What are the reasons?
4. What don't they like about their job? What are the reasons?
5. How do they see the industry developing or changing in the future?
6. What advice would they offer a new person to get started?

The answer to these questions will give you a lot of insight into the industry and help you decide whether to pursue your dream. Don't decide until you have conducted a personal interview. This can save you years of personal experience, to come to the same conclusions an interview would generate. You'll also need to examine the personal bias of the person you are interviewing. If they are at the end of their career and find the computerization of their job frustrating, this could slant their view of the career path you've chosen.

The Differences between a Wish and a Goal Are Plans

You took notes in class. Have you made notes on your life? You need to write this stuff down. Post 'em where you can see 'em. Are you comfortable with your goal and these steps?

Getting through the process of selecting your goal can easily take a week. Should you take longer, you'll have more information to base your decision upon. Decide based on reason, and you'll be a better decision maker.

There is another complication needing to be tackled. Most jobs require experience. Seeing an ad that doesn't require experience is rare. Yet you can't get the experience unless you have the job. Which came first, the chicken or the egg? Training programs, apprenticeships, and internships are the ways around this problem. If you come up against this problem, you need to do some research into what the industry expects of entry-level workers. Somehow, people get the experience and get hired for these jobs.

I have three suggestions:
1. Talk to people working in the industry and find out how they got their experience.
2. One excellent way to get the experience is to join a branch of the military. They take untrained individuals and train them. You'll get impeccable training, experience, a work history, and confidence to tackle difficult jobs successfully.
3. The other approach is to gain experience in an allied field. You'll show time on your resume doing something very similar or comparable. If your experience is that close, you may find people employed in the industry who have a similar background.

Once you've established a goal, you need to write a plan of how you are going to get there. The exercise for this chapter is to do just that: write down your goal and the steps you need to achieve your goal. Four or five steps are probably all you will need to achieve any goal. First, you must determine what your status is in relationship to the position. Then what you would have to do to qualify for the position. The final step would be applying for a position. Use the following format for your plan. Fill in the details that will work for you and your goal and try and number the steps in the order you will undertake them.

Exercise 24: Sketch out Your Plan
1. No need to get too detailed at this point.
2. Should be about a half page in length.

Here in Exercise 25 is where you make the difference between a wish and a goal. Put the date down in your notebook for this one. Answer the following questions:

Exercise 25: The Plan, First Draft
1. What is your career goal?
2. What are your educational goals?
3. What is your training/skills goals?
4. How are you going to get the experience goals?
5. When will you do a job search?
6. What is your planned career path?

This is your plan. As you refine the plan, details reveal themselves. As you move along achieving your goal, parts of your plan will become clearer to you. On your initial completion of this assignment, topics/steps can be very general. Education goals could be to graduate from college or go to graduate or business school. If your educational goals are satisfied, then mark them as achieved. Otherwise, an advanced degree (or certificate) in your planned field could be very beneficial and may be all you need to be hired. The Job Search/Placement is the point where you are making your first move into the industry, knowing you have the education, experience, and training goals completed. The Career Path is where you write down how you are going to become the CEO from starting in the mail room.

Reexamine Limitations

In setting your goal, you bump up against limitations. To set a real goal, one that will get you up every morning brimming with energy and filled with excitement, you ignore limitations. Your plan deals with the limitations. All you must do is execute the plan.

Suppose in setting your goal, you discover that a position requires many years of specialized education and many years of experience. You are unable presently to satisfy those requirements. This means going back to school and possibly having to take calculus again. Do you remember the last time you took a math course? You are not looking forward to this occasion. Are you going to let a tough course stop you from achieving your goal? When you were a kid taking a course, all you needed was a grade. Your determination wasn't in the game. This time, you've got a real goal sitting out there just out of reach. You'd be surprised how much a difference dedication and applying yourself makes in learning a course. You set a different standard for yourself, and you can drive yourself harder. Frivolous issues won't distract you, and you can home in on lessons faster than a bumblebee can find honey. What you'll discover, as many adult learners do, is the limitations you've set for yourself are not accurate. Those limitations are based on an old model for a younger person who was not as motivated as you are now.

Let's take the athletic model. There are sports where an older athlete can compete in better than a teenager. They are smarter and more knowledgeable. In baseball, managers are normally older players who remember what works. If a batter is up who will hit a ball to left on an inside pitch, they shift the outfield to take advantage of this knowledge; then they have the pitcher throw pitches inside. Consider learning as a sport. Learning becomes easier as you get older. You have a broader knowledge base. You can interpret the information easier because you've employed the rationale before in a different situation.

The key to this chapter is action. You must take the first step. Your assignment for this chapter is to look at your plan, decide what the first step is, and undertake that task. If your task is an educational goal, visit the school or training company's web page, or call up to request a brochure be sent to you. Step up to the plate and take a swing, batter, because you are about to connect.

Exercise 26: Activate the Plan
1. Today, I initiated my plan by…
2. My next step is…

No-Limits Living
Suppose you want to be a nuclear physicist, but you don't have a PhD in physics. What do you have to do to get one? Put those steps into the plan. They are just hoops you must jump through.

There are plans and then there are plans. I was amazed to discover how long you must study to get a PhD. They are quite knowledgeable in a narrow field. But if there are no jobs in their field, they are in the same boat you are.

For some reason, employers have this thing about education. They think if you are educated, then you are going to leave for a better job, or you might tell them how to do their job. Both could be true. There is little you can do for an employer who believes this. You're not going to pretend to be stupid. If they don't want to hire you based on *who you are* and *what you can do for them*, that's their tough luck. If you get mad, you can start up a competitor and drive them out of business. After I retired from the phone company, I can remember applying for jobs I could do in my sleep. I never heard from them. I thought this strange, but if they don't talk to you, they'll never find out what you could do for them.

I mentioned in the last chapter, your plan might need some refinement. Let's talk about this for a minute. As you begin implementing your plan, you will be getting more and more detailed information. When the plan is in the conceptualization phase, these details are cumbersome and are overlooked. You need to keep your eye on the goal. Getting caught up in the details may not allow you to formulate your plan on the grand scale. but, at some point, they need to be considered. *This is that point.*

Your plan needs room for the details. Suppose in the educational component of your plan, you need to apply to a certain school. This means you'll have to send for your diplomas from previous schools you've attended. These chores don't need to be written down in the plan, but they do need to be accomplished. You could start a list incidental to your plan. This supplemental list would consist of job details that need to be taken care of to accomplish your goal in life. If your plan is thorough, you will have made allowance for these details to take place. There are no limits on what you intend to tackle, but there could be a time consideration. I have a suggestion to help you.

As an exercise for this chapter, review your plan and write some details not on your plan but need to be accomplished for the plan to succeed. The tasks could be something as simple as to call an acquaintance who works in one of the fields you are interested in. If you are my age, put down what you are going to the library for! You'll be goal driven to accomplish just the tasks you've assigned and not waste time.

Exercise 27: To-Do List

1.
2.
3.

You may notice there is nothing listed. That's your job. Cross off the items as you accomplish them. Only put on the list what you want to accomplish in one day (today). You don't throw the list out until everything is crossed off. You can start a new list before finishing the current list but hang onto the uncompleted list. At some point, these lingering items should be evaluated. A digital to-do list app called QuickMemo+ is available on smartphones.

And the Bible Says…
Jesus himself uses the jump-through-the-hoop allegory when He compares the task for a rich man to get into heaven to a camel trying to pass through the eye of a needle. Keep this in mind when you set your goal. A successful and happy man has riches beyond money.

Please remember if your goal is to get a job just to make money, you are going to miss a lot in your life. You need money to live, but after that there are many more qualities much more important than the clothes you are wearing, the car you are driving, or the home or neighborhood you live in. If we want to know how much you are worth, we'd just sum up all your assets (what you own). But you are more valuable than just the sum of your properties. Values are one of your most important assets, but they have no monetary worth. If you have value to an employer, he'll hire you and pay you because you are worth the expense. This value proposition is one of the basic underpinnings of the American business world.

Where do you get value? At schools you get value from learning skills you can use when employed. At church you get value from the meaning of life. Churches give this information away free. All you have to do is sit there and listen. Eventually, as you get familiar with the stories, your understanding of them will improve, and you'll find more meaning in what is being communicated that applies to your situation today.

I'm going to give you another story from the New Testament to illustrate my point. Jesus was visiting a home and talking with a group of people. Martha and Mary were there as aides to the hosts when Mary stopped helping Martha and started listening to what Jesus had to say. Martha was so annoyed with Mary she complained to Jesus and asked him to tell Mary to do her chores. Jesus told Martha that Mary had decided to put first in her life what needed to be tended the most, not the needs of the assembled guests, and he had no problem with Mary—nor should Martha. Mary's value was exemplified in this reordering of priorities.

The exercise for this chapter focuses on your priorities in life. Question 2 asks for an example of where you prioritized and put one value over another. Turning down overtime to be with your family would be one example.

Exercise 28: What Are Your Priorities?
1. What do you value?
2. Provide an example of an occasion when you rearranged some activities to allow for something more important in your life.
3. By the way, is everything on your to-do list pointed to your goal, or are errands and favors getting in the way?

Create Opportunities

Four points: Keep your friends. Make new friends. Go where the action is. Go with the flow.

Once you've put your plan into action, you need to expand its scope. There is an intrinsic value to your involvement. You are different because you are acting upon your plan. People will notice. You have a different view about your time. You have different interests than before. Not all your friends will be happy about that. You are going to make something of yourself. If they are real friends, they'll be happy for you. If you are more interesting and have found some meaning in your life and a purpose, their friendship with you will become more meaningful to them. Your friends will encourage you. Some people will not be happy with your plans because your changing makes them feel insecure. They are more comfortable with a static relationship with no threat to the status quo or themselves.

Life tells us that change is inevitable. You will be in a position to take advantage of changes because you have a plan. You create the opportunity because you are different. If you had no plan and the same set of circumstances occurred, you wouldn't take advantage of the opportunity because you weren't ready to take any action. The opportunity would slip by unnoticed.

The exercise for this chapter is for you to discuss your plan with one or two friends and get their opinions. Record their suggestions in your notebook.

Exercise 29: Soliciting Advice

1. Name of person and their opinion/suggestion.

A Short Story about Keeping Friends
When I was a young man in high school and wanted to learn to swim, I went to the high school pool for the lessons. Later, even though I could barely swim, I tried out for the water polo team. Eventually, I was a goalie on a championship team because I could tread water. I didn't need to swim that well, just tread water. I was part of a team and still correspond regularly with some of the team members. We still keep cheering each other on.

In this story, I didn't have much to contribute, but the part I did contribute was very valuable. I didn't have the talent and skill of the best player. In fact, I was probably the worst player. But I could play goalie well. That skill was valuable to the team. In work, not everyone is a star player, but we all contribute. Don't underestimate yourself because your skills are not star quality or as good as someone else, especially those who have many years of experience. You only need a certain level of proficiency to be useful. You'll have plenty of time to work on improving your skills, and good employers are aware of this aspect.

Everyone needs a cheering squad. There are times when you get discouraged about your life and your job, and especially when looking for a job. In a demanding job, sometimes months can pass before you can start contributing to the work of the team, even though you've been trying since day one. The team will notice.

My assignment for you in this chapter is to call up an old friend you haven't seen or heard from in a long while and find out what they are up to. Enjoy the call and their friendship. Because this is an assignment, write down whom you called and what their plans are. Mention your plans to them as well. When you get good at this, what you learn from their plans will make your plan better. That is a free bonus of this exercise.

Exercise 30: Reaching out to Friends

1. Name of friend called
2. What their plans are
3. What you learned from them

You'll probably notice when you call people you haven't spoken to in a while, there have been lots of changes in their lives. Notice how much of an emphasis they place on their family as opposed to their job or some activity you both might have in common. When you mentioned your plans, did they have any suggestions? You could go back and add their suggestions to Exercise 29, "Soliciting Advice."

A Longer Story about Making New Friends

When I was a bit older, I wanted to become a microwave technician but needed an FCC license. When I started to study for the exam, I realized no one I knew talked about radio frequencies or could answer my questions. I visited the radio department at my company and met some of the radio technicians on the job. I visited them often at lunch while learning about their skill set, and they answered most of my questions. They even liked me being around because I gave them the opportunity to explain what they were doing. I eventually wound up working with them. They were all ham radio operators. I joined a ham radio club and made some lifetime friends there. One of these friends was a professional engineer who recommended me for my professional engineer's license.

The lesson in this chapter is obvious: make new friends in your new career. How can you do that? Friendship is built upon trust and caring. To begin a friendship, you must extend yourself, which begins with an introduction. Over time and many exchanges comes meaning. The meaning is built up from numerous exchanges and moments of sharing. Value is what you place upon this meaning. I value my friends' relationships because they bring meaning to my life.

The assignment here is obvious: make a new friend who can help you out in your new career. To do that you'll have to create an opportunity. You'll need to meet them. This part is a bit tough because you never know how to start up a relationship. Here is my suggestion: visit a location where people who are actively engaged in your career work and ask to take a tour. By the time you reach this stage of the plan, you'll be somewhat knowledgeable about the work they do and be able to ask good questions. Somebody will take an interest in helping you. Make sure you remember their name and ask them for their business card.

Exercise 31: Making New Friends

1. Date, the person you met, where, and what you learned
2. What was the follow-up?

Where Are the Jobs?

To take advantage of an opportunity, you must be involved. Join a society, club, or professional group related to your goals. Visit job fairs and trade shows. Read the trade magazines, as they have serious employment ads in them. Talk to everyone. Find out how they got their job.

This is the expansion portion of your plan. You are taking the creation of opportunities quite to heart, and you are ruthlessly campaigning. Don't be content with making a friend with someone in the industry; you are now out looking for groups where these people all gather under one roof on social occasions. That's the purpose of societies and clubs. These organizations support their members and allow them to get to know each other and share ideas.

The first part of your assignment is to look up a society or interest group for people employed in this industry might join. Find out what their requirements for membership are. The second part of your assignment is to read a trade magazine people employed in this career might read. A good place to find a source of these magazines is in the waiting room of the place of employment where you are being interviewed. See if there are any ads for a convention or trade show. Use your smartphone to take photos of the ads. You can also use the internet to research this information. Finally, write down what you found out in this exercise.

You might have discovered a convention is being held nearby or a local meeting is coming up. Make a note of who is advertising in these magazines. These are possible employers. Many of these magazines include assessments/outlooks/projections for the future of the industry, trends, and other articles of interest to people employed in the industry. Trade magazines are a wealth of current information.

Exercise 32: Expansion Plans

1. List the interest groups you have discovered.
2. List trade magazines you are going to sign up for.
3. Have you joined LinkedIn?
4. Have you filled out your profile on LinkedIn?
5. Have you checked LinkedIn for friends yet?
6. How is LinkedIn different from Facebook?
7. Did you know employers check LinkedIn and other social media for information, good and bad, about applicants?

Where Did the Jobs Go?
Nobody's hiring. If you don't change, employers will find workers with H-1B visas. Ever think of offering your services for a fee? Starting your own business? You can go back to the same companies that didn't hire you and do business. Keep this option in mind.

At some point, you may get very, very frustrated. You can take a low-paying job to make ends meet, but that often limits your ability to be available for an opportunity. To break out of the mold, many people try to work themselves up the corporate ladder. For a job well done, you should be rewarded, and a promotion is part and parcel of the routine. But in this case, we're talking about a ladder that may have disappeared. The safe route was on the ladder or a similar one in about the same spot or higher. What I am suggesting is for you to make your own ladder and put yourself at the top. Then, you don't have to waste time with office politics or climbing a ladder, and you can really concentrate on what you do best.

In the exercise for this chapter, I'd like you to consider your leadership potential. Write down an example or two of when you took charge and were successful in bring closure to a project of some nature. If you are seriously considering this alternative, a good resource to consider is the Small Business Administration for advice from their SCORE (www.score.org) program.

Exercise 33: Leadership Examples
1. List several instances where you demonstrated leadership, what your role was, and what the results were. Be aware that during an interview, you may want to emphasize one instance over another.

This chapter is for the older worker. Discrimination by age is illegal but getting the Equal Employment Opportunity Commission to prosecute is an arduous process. If this law is being flouted, ask yourself: What other shortcuts is this business taking?

Be prepared to fill a binder full of resumes and job descriptions. I'd suggest revising your resume to include some of the information from the above exercise. By applications of the principles expounded upon in this book, you will find that job.

What's This about Going with the Flow?
Ever notice when water is flowing downhill, it backs up until a way is found around an obstruction? Times and needs change. Jobs change. People change. Right now, employers are trying to hold onto employees to ride the recession out. If you can't get a job in your field, take the job that's there.

When you found a trade magazine I mentioned a few pages back, check the back for employment ads. Again, these are serious ads, and you'll have to be well along in your plan to apply. You'll probably notice not all the ads are for the same type of position. But the ad appears in the trade magazine for the industry. The people placing the ad could be looking for people from that industry to work in an allied field possibly or in a business servicing the industry of your interest. Answering this ad could be an opportunity to get experience that you can use. If there is a path in one direction between the two careers, most likely the path goes the other way also.

Your assignment for this chapter is to answer one of the ads. Find out if the position is still available. Please be aware there are some ads in the papers simply to satisfy a legal requirement for a company to advertise. If the ad is from an employment or recruiting agency, they will probably give you some idea of the possibility of an opening in your field. They might tell you that you do not have the qualification for the job. To satisfy this assignment, you need to come away from the conversation with some knowledge about your career and what the prospects are.

Some businesses contract out to employment agencies to find employees. They may not be large enough to have a human resources department. In a sense, the agencies are gatekeepers. You shouldn't be wary of them, but if you find you are not getting through to the employers, you're wasting your time. Agencies sift through applicants and only refer a few over to the actual employer, who then conducts their own interviews. They need a lot of applicants to sell their services to the employers. You can be cannon fodder for them; then again, you might get lucky. You're better off going to interviews from your state employment service because the businesses who list their jobs with the state have positions that they want filled. Businesses who list with agencies tend to want an "ideal" candidate.

A few words about business employment cycles might be helpful. Before a recession, businesses adapt by slimming down their workforce. During a recession they try to hold onto their employees to ride the tough times out. After a recession, they expand their workforce to take advantage of the increased business opportunities. Being hired is not impossible before and during a recession, but you need to be aware there are lots of candidates competing for the same position. The question you need to ask yourself that is valid in any employment cycle is this: *What makes me stand out?*

Exercise 34: First Contact

Make a list of positions advertised and inquired about.
1. What was the position advertised you looked up? Record the phone number or website.
2. Did you speak to anyone about the position? List the name.
3. Did you submit an application?
4. Is the position something you could do?
5. How did the conversation end?
6. What's your next step?

If the Part Is Broken, There Are Choices...
A technician can replace the part. An engineer has two choices: fix the reason the part broke or find a different way to do the same job better. In your case, you can: 1) make no changes, or 2) go back to school and improve yourself. You've been there, done that; now you're going to try something different.

I'm making an argument here for you to get more than just another job. You need to be working on your career. A career is equal to the sum of all your jobs.

No one job is critical, but they all have a theme, distinct because of what you brought to your jobs. Your contribution to society could be summed up in your career. The exercise in this chapter is to get you thinking about what makes you special on the job to help you identify your career. For students without any job experience, think of individual courses as your job. You had to show up on time, take notes, turn in homework, perform tests, and analyze and make sense of the material.

Exercise 35: Career Analysis

1. Name one skill common to all your jobs.
2. What aspects do your jobs have in common?
3. What was easiest for you to do on any job?
4. What did you like doing the best?
5. What were your plans (what's next)?
6. If someone were to ask you what you did for a living, what would you tell them?

Never Say No

Part of creating opportunities is being able to take advantage of them. Serendipity (coincidence) happens if you are available. People can't come in if the door is closed. You can't "afford" to say no.

There is a saying, opportunity never knocks twice. Let me give you this visual: your plan has put you in the driver's seat of a taxicab called opportunity; you only need to pull over to pick up the fares. You don't necessarily know where they will be, but you have your eye out for them. Being unemployed has given you the freedom to be able to go through any open door. You can even choose which one you'd like to go through. You'll want as many open doors as possible.

We need an exercise which will allow you to experience serendipity. Pick a day, a full day, like tomorrow, where you won't say the word "no" to anyone. You will agree to anything. Go to meetings, go on interviews, go to the store, or stay home. Whatever is on the schedule; for that day, the schedule is going to bend if someone asks you to change your plans or do something for them. You do have to be around people for this exercise to work. You might even try creating the opportunity by asking someone what their plans are for the day then asking to tag along or meet them later. At the end of the day, ask yourself: What was different about the day? What one thing occurred you would have missed if you had said no to a course of action?

Exercise 36: Serendipity Experiment
1. Who did I meet whom I had never met before?
2. What did I do I've never done before?
3. Where I went, I had never been before?
4. What did I learn today that was new?
5. What started this chain of events?
6. Was this an adventure?

Life Isn't Planned
Affirmation of life is the gift and the freedom to say yes. We can set our goals and make our plans, but life happens. Enjoying what happens is the best way to say yes.

You may have enjoyed your experiment with serendipity so much you may want to repeat the exercise again. Since you weren't using the word *no* for the experiment, you might have noticed you were using the word *yes* more often. You could reflect on how much easier life could be if you always say yes to everyone.

No one gives you an easy path through life. You make decisions about where and with whom you are involved. You have an adult's knowledge and wisdom which you use to make decisions. The experiment with serendipity was just that: an experiment. The purpose was to help you realize the numerous opportunities that abound if we let them. Life will throw us challenges and ask us to adjust. There is opportunity for growth and change if we let life happen around us. The realization of an unexpected happening, and that you are involved, can make for an enjoyable event. You are executing your plan, letting serendipity occur, and saying yes more often. Your assignment for this chapter is to keep track of how many times you say yes today or for the whole week.

Exercise 37: Affirmation Action
1. Whom did you say *yes* to?
2. What you said *yes* to?
3. What happened?
4. Increment the count.
5. Repeat.

Enjoy
Being prepared to take advantage of life to achieve your goal is a win-win situation. If you don't achieve the goal, you enjoyed your life. If you do achieve your goal, you double the enjoyment.

Ever go to a movie and enjoy a story not about exceptional people, occurrences, or events but about everyday things? Hollywood can take an everyday occurrence, focus in on what is special about the event giving meaning to the film.

You don't always need Hollywood for that to happen. You are writing your own script. You just need the Hollywood effect: *lights, camera, action*. The filming starts the moment you wake up. You are the star. The best part is you don't have to wait around in a trailer to do the scene where the star cooks breakfast (or memorize lines). Plus, you don't have to do the scene over because you're a one-take guy. Nor do you have to go on tour and sit in a chair for five minutes and talk about how great your movie is. You don't have to sell anybody on your movie. Yours hasn't stopped rolling.

We haven't talked about your plan in a while because you should be making it happen. You should, by this time, be well underway to achieving your goal. In the meantime, your life is happening, and you are a participant actively looking to put into play some part of your plan.

One of my favorite movies is *Groundhog Day*. The story is about a TV weatherman, actor Bill Murray, who keeps repeating a day over and over until he becomes a human capable of having meaningful relationships. One scene is particularly insightful; he catches a kid falling out of a tree then complains the boy never thanks him, but he never stops catching him. Our lives are very much like the one Bill Murray portrayed. Many of the people in our lives we'll see again and again. In the movie, Bill Murray had the opportunity to bring new meaning every day because he could change what he brought to the same situation over and over. You can too! To quote a familiar saying: *Today is the first day of the rest of your life.*[1]

Your exercise for this chapter is to change a relationship for the better. This will make you a better person and a better employee for a prospective employer.

In this exercise, I'd really like you to go out of your way to answer the following questions by bring more meaning and value to a relationship.

Exercise 38: Bring Change to a Relationship
1. Whom did you affect?
2. What did you do?
3. What were the results?

---

[1] Charles Dederich, 1913–1997, founder of Synanon, a drug rehab program in California.

Focus

You can take any job and make yourself a success there. Once you get the job, your training and skills will provide you the opportunity to try something new. All great executives start out in the mail room.

While you're busy making yourself a better person and a potentially great employee, the bills have kept rolling in. If you need a temporary job to keep the household together while your plan unfolds, you get one. This process of implementing your plan will take some time, and you shouldn't expect the world's demands on you to lessen. You'll need to contribute your time and energy to a variety of projects. Make sure your plan doesn't get put off. Prioritize your commitments. If you must study so many hours a week to stay up with a class, you'll have to cut something out to make room.

When I decided to become a radio technician in the phone company, I was playing chess several hours a day. This was fun and I enjoyed playing the games. I took a year to wean myself away from a habit of visiting a park in New York every day to play chess. I needed to spend those hours studying instead. I still like to play chess, but I achieved my goal in life first.

Your assignment for this chapter is to list your daily activities. Account for your day hour by hour. Take a typical day, and then revise the schedule to maximize the time you spend on an activity that helps you achieve your goal.

Exercise 39: Scheduling Your Life
1. How many different tasks did you accomplish?
2. How many tasks were interrupted?
3. Were you able to get done what you wanted to accomplish today?

Details—Resume

Before anything happens, a resume must be written. Statements contained within must be verifiable. The resume is a summary of your skills and a platform for your future.

The resume is what you were. It should show an earnest person who has sought or is seeking to advance themselves by education and practical learning through on-the-job training. Some jobs have a trainee position where, at a reduced salary, you become proficient at skills essential to handle the job. Employers are looking to make you a member of their team. Their question is always this: Will you make a good team member and contribute to their success?

When you describe yourself on a resume, you need to cover topics essential to identify you:

Your background
Your experience
Your education
Your interests
Your goals

While there are no two resumes the same, there are a lot of similarities between resumes submitted for the same position. These are called keywords. Many companies use software to scan and read applicant's resumes to help filter out applicants. They use keywords. If your resume doesn't use the right keywords, you may not get a call or email back.

For this exercise, examine your resume for what looks to you like a keyword, such as, the name of positions you've applied for, positions you've held, training received, degrees, interests, and goals.

Exercise 40: List of Keywords

1. List the selected keywords from your resume.
2. Leave room for additional columns.

How do you get the right keywords if yours are not passing muster? The advertisement listing the position contains quite a few keywords. The keywords from your resume need to pretty much match those of the ad. They don't all have to match, as your interests, positions, and goals are not part of the advertisement. Those are the keywords that distinguish you from the rest of the pack and help promote your resume to the selected pile for further review.

Additionally, there is something called a long-tailed keyword, which is a keyword with adjectives attached that makes it unique. Those are very specific keywords.

For this exercise you will use the internet to help you out. Find a free keyword evaluation web page. Some pages rank the keywords for more occurrences. Here is one link: https://kwfinder.com/features/.

Exercise 41: Keyword Finder

1. Using the spare column from the previous exercise, enter your keywords on the search function of the website to discover multiple, comparable keywords.
2. List the alternate keywords next to the test keyword from your resume.

Exercise 42: Resume Editing

1. Working with a copy (not the original) of your original resume, edit the document using alternate keywords.
2. Does the resume say the same things differently?
3. Do the changes make the resume better or worse?

For the writing of a resume, I would suggest using any of the resume templates that appeal to you found in Microsoft's new templates and document suggestions (where you click on the blank document). Even better is to search online for: *interactive* resume, resume builder, or resume constructor. This allows you to get expert help for free. Check out *www.resumenerd.com*. Getting interactive assistance may well be worth the investment. This sort of assistance is something you can't get out of a book and represents an evolution in coaching/assisting students.

The idea is to create a resume that works for you and presents you in a positive manner for further review. Keep in mind, a resume is a platform or springboard for what you can become.

Details—Interviews

The focus here is looking at details related to a job search. Interviews are part of the job search. They can be over the phone, online, or in person. If you don't get to an interview, your resume could be the reason.

The human resources department is the gatekeeper for the hiring process for companies. If your resume gets you to an interview, you are in the door. You get a chance to look around and ask questions. Human resources filters the candidates for the decision makers whom you haven't yet met. The second round is where your interview skills will get you the job. Here are some helpful hints:

1. Never argue with the interviewer, but you can say: "Perhaps I didn't explain that right," or, even better, "I think you're right; thanks for bringing it up."
2. Silence your phone during the interview(s).
3. Never talk about:
    a. Video games.
    b. Politics.
    c. Religion.
    d. Negative items about past employers.
    e. Some difficulty in your life you are facing.
4. Don't:
    a. Talk too long about anything.
    b. Let your past failures distract you from the future in front of you.
    c. Chew gum or miss an interview.
    d. Slouch in the chair or look distracted.
    e. Fail to have an answer as to why you left your last employer.

Exercise 43: Your Last Job

1. Provide three acceptable answers as to why you left your last position.

Here are some interview positives:

1. Smile and greet the interviewer. Introduce yourself and use their name.
2. After you sit down and you've had a moment to open the conversation, tell them why you think you are the person for this position.
3. Phrases to use:
    a. "What a great opportunity!"
    b. "I'd be happy to work here."
4. While reviewing past positions, point out how they helped prepare you for this position.
5. Mention anyone that you know or have met who works for this company and seems happy in their job in glowing terms.
6. Dress appropriately for the position advertised.
7. Listen attentively and smile.
8. Have at least three questions for the interviewer. One legitimate question is: "What is the compensation?"
9. Thank them for their time at the end of the interview.
10. Write a short follow-up letter/email to clear up anything or just to thank them *again*.

Exercise 44: Questions for the Interviewer

1. Write three questions for the interviewer you could ask.

Before going to an interview or taking a phone interview, research the company in anticipation of their question: What attracted you to apply for this position? Be prepared to speak comfortably about their company, its products, and its people.

Exercise 45: Why This Company?

1. List the platitudes.

Stay Focused
Anything worth doing takes time, skill, and learning. You'll always get a feeling of pride in its accomplishment. Beware of distractions, but give of your time to family and society. Enjoy.

The schedule you filled out in the last chapter is quite challenging. It forces you to look at the various demands being made on your time. To bring meaning to a relationship means spending some time just on that relationship. You could be working on a project together, building a tree house, or playing a game, but everything takes time. One evening a week involved in a community or church committee is a generous amount of time to donate to help. Your plan will need some protection from good causes that want your time. If you are ahead of schedule in implementing your plan, you could divert some time to a good cause; otherwise, you'll have to say no. And every time you say no, you are closing the door on opportunities. Life is a juggling act. You'll find as your plan becomes more and more successful, you'll have less and less time to implement it. People will become aware of how good you are and will make more and more demands on your time. They enjoy having you around, and you enjoy being there. But occasionally, you must go off and pay attention to what will make you a success: keeping your plan revised and focused on its attainment.

The exercise for this chapter consists of making a revision of your initial plan. If you have not done so already, incorporate new ideas about yourself and your goals that you have become aware of since undertaking a reading of this book. This exercise is not easy because it incorporates the information you gathered in the previous chapters into your plan.

Exercise 46: What Is My Plan Today?

1. Career goals:
2. Educational goals:
3. Training goals:
4. Background/experience goals:
5. Job search/placement:
6. Career path:

If you have no prospects for employment in your chosen field, what is your backup plan? Have you considered the commuting time in your plan? Would you consider moving to an area where your prospects for employment are better? Some employers provide relocation expenses for new employees.

Changes
"The Times They Are A-Changin'"
—Song by Bob Dylan, 1963

The challenge today, especially in technology industries, is to stay on top of change while looking for a job or keeping up for the job you already have. How you manage change is your biggest criteria for success. How quickly you meet the challenge of learning the new material, technique, or software is a measure of your adaptability. You need to keep yourself informed on specific issues pertinent to your career path. A good method for getting in touch with timely information is to subscribe to a trade publication or internet blog.

What an individual needs to know today to be successful can be overwhelming. There is a glut of information, but there is no reason to not want to be a part of the ongoing evolution of life. The important of having a focus and goal in mind is to help measure the rate you are achieving success. You know what is on the horizon: your next step, but you need some understanding of potential changes happening so that you can adapt your plan. Having a solid foundation of knowledge is a good basis for interpreting change.

You should have set up a plan by now that you are intent upon or have been executing. In this chapter's exercise, I have a few questions that will challenge you.

Exercise 47: Changes

1. How are you handling the changes that occurred in your industry while you were on this job search?
2. Can you identify what these changes are?
3. What aspect of your knowledge base has become outdated?
4. How can you demonstrate to the employer that you have current knowledge?
5. What is the source of your information about potential changes?

A System Solution

Let's do a quick review here of what we've covered. After a lot of work, we've defined ourselves, redefined our goal, set a plan in motion, and then discovered the goal is a moving target. Is this fair? Should the world stop revolving while we get our act together? What we need is a method of assessing our progress.

How would an engineer solve this problem? He'd use a feedback loop. In a strictly technical problem, **inputs** are taken in through a **buffer** which filters out all but the essential information needed to accomplish a task. The next stage could consist of an **amplifier**, where the work of the system takes place. Then finally, there is the **output**, the finished product. The system takes a sample of the results and feeds that information back into the buffer for comparison purposes called **feedback**. The major parts of a feedback system are shown in the diagram below.

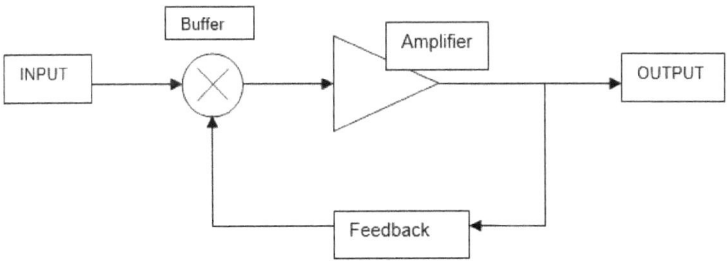

The same system *redefined* can be used to evaluate and modify your plan. The control input is the plan you've evolved to put you back to work. The signal is your resume, consisting of your work history and any preparation you've made, such as schooling or job training. The overall goal can be broken up into intermediate steps in the buffer. The buffer is where the evaluation is done, and tasks are added to the to-do list. The amplifier is where the work gets done and tasks are accomplished. The output is where you stand after finishing a task. The feedback is your estimation or assessment of whether you've achieved your goal. For example, if your plan included finishing up your college degree, the output, one college degree, would thus modify the input to this system. The work of achieving your goal would now be modified to reflect this changed status, that task gets crossed off the list. The changed status is incorporated into your overall goal by selecting another task. This is what the system looks like with this understanding of the functions:

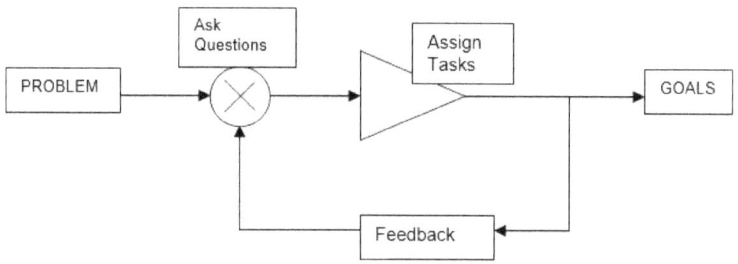

This same system for refining your plan has other applications—for example, learning. Learning is a process where you invoke a system of inquiry:

Ask questions
Break into tasks
Set goals
Feedback
Evaluation

For this chapter's exercise, you'll look at some previous actions and justify the reasons you made for one decision over another. In the systems approach, this is part of the evaluation process that goes on in the buffer section. Then, based upon your evaluation, you assign tasks to the to-do list. This is a crucial part of the system: incorporating new tasks based upon a changed situation.

Exercise 48: Evaluation

1. What were the reasons you picked one career/job over another in Exercises 19 and 20?
2. What were the reasons you took the advice of one person over another in Exercise 26?

By using the system approach, getting a job is like whittling down a square peg to fit into a round hole. We need to get a better fit as we go through a process of trial and error. Even when everything seems to fit, with better preparation, success becomes easier. This is what you'll be doing with your plan as you process through your job search. Some advice and decisions are taken because they align you better with the desired goal.

While we have come to the end of this book, you may not have achieved your desired position yet. Time will reveal an outcome from your work that may please you. Your learning will go on, and opportunities will come your way. Often, when you reach one plateau, by stopping and looking around another plateau is seen to be within reach. Your opportunities to excel are endless, and it's your decision where to go next.

Summary: Six Steps to a Paycheck

Step 1. You examine yourself from many different perspectives and have confidence in your abilities.

Step 2. You evaluate your professional goals and what you want to do in your life.

Step 3. You examine what's standing between you and your goal and start making plans.

Step 4. You increase your opportunities by expanding your horizons.

Step 5. Everyone experiences serendipity (opportunities) every day. You stand ready to take advantage of them.

Step 6. Keep your eye on the sparrows. They are fast, change direction quickly, and get smaller in the distance. You need to keep your focus and not lose track of the goal you seek.

The first three steps are to help you develop the plan to achieve your goal. The last three steps are how to go about enacting the plan successfully.

List of Exercises

Exercise 1: Describe Your Favorite Person 5
Exercise 2: Self-Description 6
Exercise 3: Talking about Feelings 11
Exercise 4: Talking about the Past 13
Exercise 5: Abilities and Skills (For the Graduate) ... 17
Exercise 6: Abilities and Skills (For the Worker) 19
Exercise 7: Negatives 21
Exercise 8: Identifying Traits (Three Columns) 25
Exercise 9: What's New 28
Exercise 10: What's New, Continued 28
Exercise 11: What's Your Experience? 29
Exercise 12: Your Abilities and Skills 30
Exercise 13: What Are You Doing Now? 30
Exercise 14: Identifiable Traits 31
Exercise 15: Life Assessments, Part 1 33
Exercise 16: Life Assessments, Part 2 34
Exercise 17: Life Assessments, Part 3 34
Exercise 18: Life Assessments, Part 4 35
Exercise 19: Revised Traits 36
Exercise 20: Make a Wish 39
Exercise 21: Career Comparison 42
Exercise 22: Job Comparison 43
Exercise 23: Personal Interview 44
Exercise 24: Sketch out Your Plan 46
Exercise 25: The Plan, First Draft 46
Exercise 26: Activate the Plan 50
Exercise 27: To-Do List 52
Exercise 28: What Are Your Priorities? 54
Exercise 29: Soliciting Advice 56
Exercise 30: Reaching out to Friends 58
Exercise 31: Making New Friends 60
Exercise 32: Expansion Plans 62
Exercise 33: Leadership Examples 63
Exercise 34: First Contact 66
Exercise 35: Career Analysis 67
Exercise 36: Serendipity Experiment 70
Exercise 37: Affirmation Action 71

Exercise 38: Bring Change to a Relationship 74
Exercise 39: Scheduling Your Life 75
Exercise 40: List of Keywords 78
Exercise 41: Keyword Finder 78
Exercise 42: Resume Editing 79
Exercise 43: Your Last Job 81
Exercise 44: Questions for the Interviewer 82
Exercise 45: Why This Company? 82
Exercise 46: What Is My Plan Today? 84
Exercise 47: Changes 86
Exercise 48: Evaluation 89

About the Author

Timothy M. Johnson graduated from Fontana High School in Fontana, California, in 1964 with honors. He attended the US Merchant Marine Academy in Kings Point, New York, as a member of the class of 1968, leaving after two years to marry and live in Baltimore. He then went through a trying period of searching for a job with an incomplete college degree. He would spend most of the week searching and then would be let go after working a few days because he hadn't quite figured out the system yet. He once worked at a pawn shop for less than the minimum wage, which was, in the late sixties, only $1.25 an hour. After two months of working different jobs every week, the jobs began lasting longer, and he began leaving one job for a better job. During this period, he applied for a job with AT&T but was turned down because he didn't have a college degree. His jobs began lasting longer with better pay. His jobs were mostly with restaurants, sales, bill collection, and auto financing industries. These industries have a high turnover of personnel because they are minimum-skill-level jobs or require some college experience.

When he moved to New York to be closer to family, he found employment in the airline industry as a ramp ticket agent, which he left when he was hired by New York Telephone. They discovered he knew so much about the employment business that he never left the employment office, working his way up to be an interviewer for technical jobs. Two years later he transferred to the field where he could work with his hands. He rose through the craft ranks from unskilled to skilled employee as a radio systems technician after becoming interested in that career from his activities as a ham radio operator. He had to acquire an FCC

General License to qualify for that job. He retired from the phone company in 1994 at age forty-seven.

During his career at the phone company, he completed his undergraduate requirements at Empire State College in 1983, paid for as a company benefit. He then completed a master of arts in liberal studies at the State University of New York at Stonybrook in 1993 as preparation for obtaining a professional engineer's license. He next completed a master's degree in electrical engineering at New York Institute of Technology in 1997. Both master's degrees were paid for by the phone company. While he was studying for this second master's, he began teaching sailing at Oyster Bay Sailing School and obtained his Master License, Near Coastal, 100 tons, sitting for the US Coast Guard license exam thirty years after he initiated studies in this career path.

He moved to Massachusetts, settling in Cape Cod in 1997. He spent a year on a job search before securing a position as an industrial/research junior engineer in the Boston area. He began teaching at Wentworth Institute of Technology in Boston, Massachusetts, in 1999, becoming a full-time faculty member in 2000. At the same time, he established a consulting business called Captains Engineering Services and joined the local Rotary Club. In October of 2002, he passed the eight-hour exam for the professional engineer license in electrical engineering.

At Wentworth, he has taught over 3,300 students in elements of electronics that range from basic electronic design and circuit theory to digital circuits, VHDL, microprocessors, fiber optics, and VLSI design. He retired in 2015 to complete studies for a doctor of professional studies in computing at Pace University in New York in 2018. He now holds a technology degree, a liberal arts degree, an engineering degree, and a computer degree (some 220 college credits).

During his higher education career in Boston, he was president of the Massachusetts Society of Professional Engineers in 2004, student coordinator for IEEE clubs for the executive board of the Boston section of the IEEE, an active member of the American Society of Engineering Educations, writing and presenting papers, and a member of the Rotary Club of Bourne. He has written four books and one play. His fun job on weekends during his years in Boston was teaching sailing for Boston Harbor Sailing Club, covering subjects from basic sailing to coastal navigation courses. This experience provided the material for his book *Performance Sailing on a J29*.

Notes:

www.ingramcontent.com/pod-product-compliance
Lightning Source LLC
Chambersburg PA
CBHW050843160426
43192CB00011B/2136